MINDFULNESS
DAILY JOURNAL

MINDFULNESS DAILY JOURNAL

Date: ___/___/20___   Sun   Mon   Tue   Wed   Thu   Fri   Sat

Today I CHOOSE TO FEEL

Today's FOCUS

Today I FEEL INSPIRED BY

Today's GOOD HABITS

To Do
- ☐ _____
- ☐ _____
- ☐ _____
- ☐ _____
- ☐ _____
- ☐ _____

Self-Care

Today I'm GRATEFUL for: _____

Today (Small or Great) VICTORIES: _____

Today I LEARNED: _____

NOTES

BRAIN DUMP

What I can control

SELF-CARE IDEAS

HAPPINESS IS

MINDFULNESS DAILY JOURNAL

Date: ___/___/20___   Sun   Mon   Tue   Wed   Thu   Fri   Sat

Today I CHOOSE TO FEEL

Today's FOCUS

Today I FEEL INSPIRED BY

Today's GOOD HABITS

To Do
- ☐ _____
- ☐ _____
- ☐ _____
- ☐ _____
- ☐ _____
- ☐ _____

Self-Care
- _____
- _____
- _____
- _____
- _____
- _____

Today I'm GRATEFUL for: _____

Today (Small or Great) VICTORIES: _____

Today I LEARNED: _____

NOTES

BRAIN DUMP

What I can control

SELF-CARE IDEAS

HAPPINESS IS

MINDFULNESS DAILY JOURNAL

Date: ___/___/20___   Sun Mon Tue Wed Thu Fri Sat

Today I CHOOSE TO FEEL

Today's FOCUS

Today I FEEL INSPIRED BY

Today's GOOD HABITS

To Do
- _____
- _____
- _____
- _____
- _____
- _____
- _____

Self-Care
- -
- -
- -
- -
- -
- -

Today I'm GRATEFUL for: _____

Today (Small or Great) VICTORIES: _____

Today I LEARNED: _____

NOTES

BRAIN DUMP

What I can control

SELF-CARE IDEAS

HAPPINESS IS

MINDFULNESS DAILY JOURNAL

Date: ___/___/20___   Sun Mon Tue Wed Thu Fri Sat

Today I CHOOSE TO FEEL

Today's FOCUS

Today I FEEL INSPIRED BY

Today's GOOD HABITS

To Do
- ☐ _____
- ☐ _____
- ☐ _____
- ☐ _____
- ☐ _____
- ☐ _____

Self-Care

Today I'm GRATEFUL for: _____

Today (Small or Great) VICTORIES: _____

Today I LEARNED: _____

NOTES

BRAIN DUMP

What I can control

SELF-CARE IDEAS

HAPPINESS IS

MINDFULNESS DAILY JOURNAL

Date: ___/___/20___   Sun   Mon   Tue   Wed   Thu   Fri   Sat

Today I CHOOSE TO FEEL

Today's FOCUS

Today I FEEL INSPIRED BY

Today's GOOD HABITS

To Do
- ☐ _____
- ☐ _____
- ☐ _____
- ☐ _____
- ☐ _____
- ☐ _____

Self-Care
- _____
- _____
- _____
- _____
- _____

Today I'm GRATEFUL for: _____

Today (Small or Great) VICTORIES: _____

Today I LEARNED: _____

NOTES

BRAIN DUMP

What I can control

SELF-CARE IDEAS

HAPPINESS IS

MINDFULNESS DAILY JOURNAL

Date: ___/___/20___   Sun   Mon   Tue   Wed   Thu   Fri   Sat

Today I CHOOSE TO FEEL

Today's FOCUS

Today I FEEL INSPIRED BY

Today's GOOD HABITS

To Do

- [ ]
- [ ]
- [ ]
- [ ]
- [ ]
- [ ]

Self-Care

Today I'm GRATEFUL for: _____

Today (Small or Great) VICTORIES: _____

Today I LEARNED: _____

NOTES

BRAIN DUMP

What I can control

SELF-CARE IDEAS

HAPPINESS IS

MINDFULNESS DAILY JOURNAL

Date: ___/___/20___   Sun   Mon   Tue   Wed   Thu   Fri   Sat

Today I CHOOSE TO FEEL

Today's FOCUS

Today I FEEL INSPIRED BY

Today's GOOD HABITS

To Do

- [ ] ___
- [ ] ___
- [ ] ___
- [ ] ___
- [ ] ___
- [ ] ___

Self-Care

_____
_____
_____
_____
_____
_____

Today I'm GRATEFUL for: ___

Today (Small or Great) VICTORIES: ___

Today I LEARNED: ___

NOTES

BRAIN DUMP

What I can control

SELF-CARE IDEAS

HAPPINESS IS

MINDFULNESS DAILY JOURNAL

Date: ___/___/20___   Sun   Mon   Tue   Wed   Thu   Fri   Sat

Today I CHOOSE TO FEEL

Today's FOCUS

Today I FEEL INSPIRED BY

Today's GOOD HABITS

To Do
- ☐ _____
- ☐ _____
- ☐ _____
- ☐ _____
- ☐ _____
- ☐ _____

Self-Care
- -
- -
- -
- -
- -
- -

Today I'm GRATEFUL for: _____

_____

Today (Small or Great) VICTORIES: _____

_____

Today I LEARNED: _____

_____

NOTES

BRAIN DUMP

What I can control

SELF-CARE IDEAS

HAPPINESS IS

MINDFULNESS DAILY JOURNAL

Date: ___/___/20___   Sun   Mon   Tue   Wed   Thu   Fri   Sat

Today I CHOOSE TO FEEL

Today's FOCUS

Today I FEEL INSPIRED BY

Today's GOOD HABITS

To Do

☐ ___
☐ ___
☐ ___
☐ ___
☐ ___
☐ ___

Self-Care

Today I'm GRATEFUL for: ___

Today (Small or Great) VICTORIES: ___

Today I LEARNED: ___

NOTES

BRAIN DUMP

What I can control

SELF-CARE IDEAS

HAPPINESS IS

MINDFULNESS DAILY JOURNAL

Date: ___/___/20___   Sun   Mon   Tue   Wed   Thu   Fri   Sat

Today I CHOOSE TO FEEL

Today's FOCUS

Today I FEEL INSPIRED BY

Today's GOOD HABITS

To Do
- [ ]
- [ ]
- [ ]
- [ ]
- [ ]
- [ ]

Self-Care

Today I'm GRATEFUL for: _____

Today (Small or Great) VICTORIES: _____

Today I LEARNED: _____

NOTES

BRAIN DUMP

What I can control

SELF-CARE IDEAS

HAPPINESS IS

MINDFULNESS DAILY JOURNAL

Date: ___/___/20___   Sun Mon Tue Wed Thu Fri Sat

Today I CHOOSE TO FEEL

Today's FOCUS

Today I FEEL INSPIRED BY

Today's GOOD HABITS

To Do

- [ ]
- [ ]
- [ ]
- [ ]
- [ ]
- [ ]

Self-Care

Today I'm GRATEFUL for: _____

Today (Small or Great) VICTORIES: _____

Today I LEARNED: _____

NOTES

BRAIN DUMP

What I can control

SELF-CARE IDEAS

HAPPINESS IS

MINDFULNESS DAILY JOURNAL

Date: ___/___/20___   Sun   Mon   Tue   Wed   Thu   Fri   Sat

Today I CHOOSE TO FEEL

Today's FOCUS

Today I FEEL INSPIRED BY

Today's GOOD HABITS

To Do

☐ _____
☐ _____
☐ _____
☐ _____
☐ _____
☐ _____

Self-Care

Today I'm GRATEFUL for: _____

_____

Today (Small or Great) VICTORIES: _____

_____

Today I LEARNED: _____

_____

NOTES

BRAIN DUMP

What I can control

SELF-CARE IDEAS

HAPPINESS IS

MINDFULNESS DAILY JOURNAL

Date: ___/___/20___   Sun   Mon   Tue   Wed   Thu   Fri   Sat

Today I CHOOSE TO FEEL

Today's FOCUS

Today I FEEL INSPIRED BY

Today's GOOD HABITS

To Do

- [ ]
- [ ]
- [ ]
- [ ]
- [ ]
- [ ]

Self-Care

Today I'm GRATEFUL for: _____

Today (Small or Great) VICTORIES: _____

Today I LEARNED: _____

NOTES

BRAIN DUMP

What I can control

SELF-CARE IDEAS

HAPPINESS IS

MINDFULNESS DAILY JOURNAL

Date: ___/___/20___   Sun   Mon   Tue   Wed   Thu   Fri   Sat

Today I CHOOSE TO FEEL

Today's FOCUS

Today I FEEL INSPIRED BY

Today's GOOD HABITS

To Do
-
-
-
-
-
-

Self-Care
-
-
-
-
-
-

Today I'm GRATEFUL for: _____

Today (Small or Great) VICTORIES: _____

Today I LEARNED: _____

NOTES

BRAIN DUMP

What I can control

SELF-CARE IDEAS

HAPPINESS IS

MINDFULNESS DAILY JOURNAL

Date: ___/___/20___   Sun Mon Tue Wed Thu Fri Sat

Today I CHOOSE TO FEEL

Today's FOCUS

Today I FEEL INSPIRED BY

Today's GOOD HABITS

To Do
-
-
-
-
-
-

Self-Care

Today I'm GRATEFUL for: _____

Today (Small or Great) VICTORIES: _____

Today I LEARNED: _____

NOTES

BRAIN DUMP

What I can control

SELF-CARE IDEAS

HAPPINESS IS

MINDFULNESS DAILY JOURNAL

Date: ___/___/20___   Sun   Mon   Tue   Wed   Thu   Fri   Sat

Today I CHOOSE TO FEEL

Today's FOCUS

Today I FEEL INSPIRED BY

Today's GOOD HABITS

To Do
- ☐ _____
- ☐ _____
- ☐ _____
- ☐ _____
- ☐ _____
- ☐ _____

Self-Care

Today I'm GRATEFUL for: _____

Today (Small or Great) VICTORIES: _____

Today I LEARNED: _____

NOTES

BRAIN DUMP

What I can control

SELF-CARE IDEAS

HAPPINESS IS

MINDFULNESS DAILY JOURNAL

Date: ___/___/20___   Sun Mon Tue Wed Thu Fri Sat

Today I CHOOSE TO FEEL

Today's FOCUS

Today I FEEL INSPIRED BY

Today's GOOD HABITS

To Do

-
-
-
-
-
-

Self-Care

Today I'm GRATEFUL for: _____

Today (Small or Great) VICTORIES: _____

Today I LEARNED: _____

NOTES

BRAIN DUMP

What I can control

SELF-CARE IDEAS

HAPPINESS IS

MINDFULNESS DAILY JOURNAL

Date: ___/___/20___   Sun   Mon   Tue   Wed   Thu   Fri   Sat

Today I CHOOSE TO FEEL

Today's FOCUS

Today I FEEL INSPIRED BY

Today's GOOD HABITS

To Do

- [ ]
- [ ]
- [ ]
- [ ]
- [ ]
- [ ]

Self-Care

Today I'm GRATEFUL for: _____

Today (Small or Great) VICTORIES: _____

Today I LEARNED: _____

NOTES

BRAIN DUMP

What I can control

SELF-CARE IDEAS

HAPPINESS IS

MINDFULNESS DAILY JOURNAL

Date: ___/___/20___   Sun Mon Tue Wed Thu Fri Sat

Today I CHOOSE TO FEEL

Today's FOCUS

Today I FEEL INSPIRED BY

Today's GOOD HABITS

To Do
-
-
-
-
-
-

Self-Care

Today I'm GRATEFUL for: _____

Today (Small or Great) VICTORIES: _____

Today I LEARNED: _____

NOTES

BRAIN DUMP

What I can control

SELF-CARE IDEAS

HAPPINESS IS

MINDFULNESS DAILY JOURNAL

Date: ___/___/20___   Sun Mon Tue Wed Thu Fri Sat

Today I CHOOSE TO FEEL

Today's FOCUS

Today I FEEL INSPIRED BY

Today's GOOD HABITS

To Do

- [ ] _____
- [ ] _____
- [ ] _____
- [ ] _____
- [ ] _____
- [ ] _____

Self-Care

Today I'm GRATEFUL for: _____

Today (Small or Great) VICTORIES: _____

Today I LEARNED: _____

NOTES

BRAIN DUMP

What I can control

SELF-CARE IDEAS

HAPPINESS IS

MINDFULNESS DAILY JOURNAL

Date: ___/___/20___   Sun   Mon   Tue   Wed   Thu   Fri   Sat

Today I CHOOSE TO FEEL

Today's FOCUS

Today I FEEL INSPIRED BY

Today's GOOD HABITS

To Do

-
-
-
-
-
-

Self-Care

Today I'm GRATEFUL for: _____

Today (Small or Great) VICTORIES: _____

Today I LEARNED: _____

NOTES

BRAIN DUMP

What I can control

SELF-CARE IDEAS

HAPPINESS IS

MINDFULNESS DAILY JOURNAL

Date: ___/___/20___   Sun   Mon   Tue   Wed   Thu   Fri   Sat

Today I CHOOSE TO FEEL

Today's FOCUS

Today I FEEL INSPIRED BY

Today's GOOD HABITS

To Do
- [ ]
- [ ]
- [ ]
- [ ]
- [ ]
- [ ]

Self-Care

Today I'm GRATEFUL for: _____

Today (Small or Great) VICTORIES: _____

Today I LEARNED: _____

NOTES

BRAIN DUMP

What I can control

SELF-CARE IDEAS

HAPPINESS IS

MINDFULNESS DAILY JOURNAL

Date: ___/___/20___   Sun   Mon   Tue   Wed   Thu   Fri   Sat

Today I CHOOSE TO FEEL

Today's FOCUS

Today I FEEL INSPIRED BY

Today's GOOD HABITS

To Do

- [ ]
- [ ]
- [ ]
- [ ]
- [ ]
- [ ]

Self-Care

Today I'm GRATEFUL for: _____

Today (Small or Great) VICTORIES: _____

Today I LEARNED: _____

NOTES

BRAIN DUMP

What I can control

SELF-CARE IDEAS

HAPPINESS IS

MINDFULNESS DAILY JOURNAL

Date: ___/___/20___   Sun   Mon   Tue   Wed   Thu   Fri   Sat

Today I CHOOSE TO FEEL

Today's FOCUS

Today I FEEL INSPIRED BY

Today's GOOD HABITS

To Do
- [ ] _____
- [ ] _____
- [ ] _____
- [ ] _____
- [ ] _____
- [ ] _____

Self-Care
- - - - - - - - - - - - - - - - - - - -
- - - - - - - - - - - - - - - - - - - -
- - - - - - - - - - - - - - - - - - - -
- - - - - - - - - - - - - - - - - - - -
- - - - - - - - - - - - - - - - - - - -
- - - - - - - - - - - - - - - - - - - -

Today I'm GRATEFUL for: _____

Today (Small or Great) VICTORIES: _____

Today I LEARNED: _____

NOTES

BRAIN DUMP

What I can control

SELF-CARE IDEAS

HAPPINESS IS

MINDFULNESS DAILY JOURNAL

Date: ___/___/20___   Sun Mon Tue Wed Thu Fri Sat

Today I CHOOSE TO FEEL

Today's FOCUS

Today I FEEL INSPIRED BY

Today's GOOD HABITS

To Do
- [ ]
- [ ]
- [ ]
- [ ]
- [ ]
- [ ]

Self-Care

Today I'm GRATEFUL for: _____

Today (Small or Great) VICTORIES: _____

Today I LEARNED: _____

NOTES

BRAIN DUMP

What I can control

SELF-CARE IDEAS

HAPPINESS IS

MINDFULNESS DAILY JOURNAL

Date: ___/___/20___   Sun Mon Tue Wed Thu Fri Sat

Today I CHOOSE TO FEEL

Today's FOCUS

Today I FEEL INSPIRED BY

Today's GOOD HABITS

To Do
-
-
-
-
-
-

Self-Care

Today I'm GRATEFUL for: _____

Today (Small or Great) VICTORIES: _____

Today I LEARNED: _____

NOTES

BRAIN DUMP

What I can control

SELF-CARE IDEAS

HAPPINESS IS

MINDFULNESS DAILY JOURNAL

Date: ___/___/20___   Sun   Mon   Tue   Wed   Thu   Fri   Sat

Today I CHOOSE TO FEEL

Today's FOCUS

Today I FEEL INSPIRED BY

Today's GOOD HABITS

To Do

- [ ] _____
- [ ] _____
- [ ] _____
- [ ] _____
- [ ] _____
- [ ] _____

Self-Care

_____
_____
_____
_____
_____
_____

Today I'm GRATEFUL for: _____

Today (Small or Great) VICTORIES: _____

Today I LEARNED: _____

NOTES

BRAIN DUMP

What I can control

SELF-CARE IDEAS

HAPPINESS IS

MINDFULNESS DAILY JOURNAL

Date: ___/___/20___   Sun   Mon   Tue   Wed   Thu   Fri   Sat

Today I CHOOSE TO FEEL

Today's FOCUS

Today I FEEL INSPIRED BY

Today's GOOD HABITS

To Do
- [ ]
- [ ]
- [ ]
- [ ]
- [ ]
- [ ]

Self-Care

Today I'm GRATEFUL for: _____

Today (Small or Great) VICTORIES: _____

Today I LEARNED: _____

NOTES

BRAIN DUMP

What I can control

SELF-CARE IDEAS

HAPPINESS IS

MINDFULNESS DAILY JOURNAL

Date: ___/___/20___   Sun Mon Tue Wed Thu Fri Sat

Today I CHOOSE TO FEEL

Today's FOCUS

Today I FEEL INSPIRED BY

Today's GOOD HABITS

To Do
- ☐ _____
- ☐ _____
- ☐ _____
- ☐ _____
- ☐ _____
- ☐ _____

Self-Care
- _____
- _____
- _____
- _____
- _____
- _____

Today I'm GRATEFUL for: _____

Today (Small or Great) VICTORIES: _____

Today I LEARNED: _____

NOTES

BRAIN DUMP

What I can control

SELF-CARE IDEAS

HAPPINESS IS

MINDFULNESS DAILY JOURNAL

Date: ___/___/20___   Sun   Mon   Tue   Wed   Thu   Fri   Sat

Today I CHOOSE TO FEEL

Today's FOCUS

Today I FEEL INSPIRED BY

Today's GOOD HABITS

To Do
-
-
-
-
-
-

Self-Care

Today I'm GRATEFUL for:

Today (Small or Great) VICTORIES:

Today I LEARNED:

NOTES

BRAIN DUMP

What I can control

SELF-CARE IDEAS

HAPPINESS IS

MINDFULNESS DAILY JOURNAL

Date: ___/___/20___   Sun   Mon   Tue   Wed   Thu   Fri   Sat

Today I CHOOSE TO FEEL

Today's FOCUS

Today I FEEL INSPIRED BY

Today's GOOD HABITS

To Do
-
-
-
-
-
-

Self-Care

Today I'm GRATEFUL for: _____

Today (Small or Great) VICTORIES: _____

Today I LEARNED: _____

NOTES

BRAIN DUMP

What I can control

SELF-CARE IDEAS

HAPPINESS IS

MINDFULNESS DAILY JOURNAL

Date: ___/___/20___   Sun Mon Tue Wed Thu Fri Sat

Today I CHOOSE TO FEEL

Today's FOCUS

Today I FEEL INSPIRED BY

Today's GOOD HABITS

To Do
- ☐ _____
- ☐ _____
- ☐ _____
- ☐ _____
- ☐ _____
- ☐ _____

Self-Care

Today I'm GRATEFUL for: _____

Today (Small or Great) VICTORIES: _____

Today I LEARNED: _____

NOTES

BRAIN DUMP

What I can control

SELF-CARE IDEAS

HAPPINESS IS

MINDFULNESS DAILY JOURNAL

Date: ___/___/20___   Sun Mon Tue Wed Thu Fri Sat

Today I CHOOSE TO FEEL

Today's FOCUS

Today I FEEL INSPIRED BY

Today's GOOD HABITS

To Do

- [ ] _____
- [ ] _____
- [ ] _____
- [ ] _____
- [ ] _____
- [ ] _____

Self-Care

_____
_____
_____
_____
_____
_____

Today I'm GRATEFUL for: _____

Today (Small or Great) VICTORIES: _____

Today I LEARNED: _____

NOTES

BRAIN DUMP

What I can control

SELF-CARE IDEAS

HAPPINESS IS

MINDFULNESS DAILY JOURNAL

Date: ___/___/20___   Sun Mon Tue Wed Thu Fri Sat

Today I CHOOSE TO FEEL

Today's FOCUS

Today I FEEL INSPIRED BY

Today's GOOD HABITS

To Do
- [ ]
- [ ]
- [ ]
- [ ]
- [ ]
- [ ]

Self-Care

Today I'm GRATEFUL for: _____

Today (Small or Great) VICTORIES: _____

Today I LEARNED: _____

NOTES

BRAIN DUMP

What I can control

SELF-CARE IDEAS

HAPPINESS IS

MINDFULNESS DAILY JOURNAL

Date: ___/___/20___   Sun   Mon   Tue   Wed   Thu   Fri   Sat

Today I CHOOSE TO FEEL

Today's FOCUS

Today I FEEL INSPIRED BY

Today's GOOD HABITS

To Do
- [ ]
- [ ]
- [ ]
- [ ]
- [ ]
- [ ]

Self-Care

Today I'm GRATEFUL for: _____

Today (Small or Great) VICTORIES: _____

Today I LEARNED: _____

NOTES

BRAIN DUMP

What I can control

SELF-CARE IDEAS

HAPPINESS IS

MINDFULNESS DAILY JOURNAL

Date: ___/___/20___   Sun   Mon   Tue   Wed   Thu   Fri   Sat

Today I CHOOSE TO FEEL

Today's FOCUS

Today I FEEL INSPIRED BY

Today's GOOD HABITS

To Do

☐ _____
☐ _____
☐ _____
☐ _____
☐ _____
☐ _____

Self-Care

- -
- -
- -
- -
- -
- -

Today I'm GRATEFUL for: _____

Today (Small or Great) VICTORIES: _____

Today I LEARNED: _____

NOTES

BRAIN DUMP

What I can control

SELF-CARE IDEAS

HAPPINESS IS

MINDFULNESS DAILY JOURNAL

Date: ___/___/20___   Sun   Mon   Tue   Wed   Thu   Fri   Sat

Today I CHOOSE TO FEEL

Today's FOCUS

Today I FEEL INSPIRED BY

Today's GOOD HABITS

To Do
- [ ]
- [ ]
- [ ]
- [ ]
- [ ]
- [ ]

Self-Care

Today I'm GRATEFUL for: _____

Today (Small or Great) VICTORIES: _____

Today I LEARNED: _____

NOTES

BRAIN DUMP

What I can control

SELF-CARE IDEAS

HAPPINESS IS

MINDFULNESS DAILY JOURNAL

Date: ___/___/20___   Sun   Mon   Tue   Wed   Thu   Fri   Sat

Today I CHOOSE TO FEEL

Today's FOCUS

Today I FEEL INSPIRED BY

Today's GOOD HABITS

To Do

- [ ]
- [ ]
- [ ]
- [ ]
- [ ]
- [ ]

Self-Care

Today I'm GRATEFUL for: _____

Today (Small or Great) VICTORIES: _____

Today I LEARNED: _____

NOTES

BRAIN DUMP

What I can control

SELF-CARE IDEAS

HAPPINESS IS

MINDFULNESS DAILY JOURNAL

Date: ___/___/20___   Sun Mon Tue Wed Thu Fri Sat

Today I CHOOSE TO FEEL

Today's FOCUS

Today I FEEL INSPIRED BY

Today's GOOD HABITS

To Do
- ☐ _____
- ☐ _____
- ☐ _____
- ☐ _____
- ☐ _____
- ☐ _____

Self-Care
- -
- -
- -
- -
- -
- -

Today I'm GRATEFUL for: _____

Today (Small or Great) VICTORIES: _____

Today I LEARNED: _____

NOTES

BRAIN DUMP

What I can control

SELF-CARE IDEAS

HAPPINESS IS

MINDFULNESS DAILY JOURNAL

Date: ___/___/20___   Sun   Mon   Tue   Wed   Thu   Fri   Sat

Today I CHOOSE TO FEEL

Today's FOCUS

Today I FEEL INSPIRED BY

Today's GOOD HABITS

To Do
- ☐ _____
- ☐ _____
- ☐ _____
- ☐ _____
- ☐ _____
- ☐ _____

Self-Care
_____
_____
_____
_____
_____
_____

Today I'm GRATEFUL for: _____

_____

Today (Small or Great) VICTORIES: _____

_____

Today I LEARNED: _____

_____

NOTES

BRAIN DUMP

What I can control

SELF-CARE IDEAS

HAPPINESS IS

MINDFULNESS DAILY JOURNAL

Date: ___/___/20___   Sun Mon Tue Wed Thu Fri Sat

Today I CHOOSE TO FEEL

Today's FOCUS

Today I FEEL INSPIRED BY

Today's GOOD HABITS

To Do
- [ ]
- [ ]
- [ ]
- [ ]
- [ ]
- [ ]

Self-Care

Today I'm GRATEFUL for:

Today (Small or Great) VICTORIES:

Today I LEARNED:

NOTES

BRAIN DUMP

What I can control

SELF-CARE IDEAS

HAPPINESS IS

MINDFULNESS DAILY JOURNAL

Date: ___/___/20___   Sun Mon Tue Wed Thu Fri Sat

Today I CHOOSE TO FEEL

Today's FOCUS

Today I FEEL INSPIRED BY

Today's GOOD HABITS

To Do

- ☐ _____
- ☐ _____
- ☐ _____
- ☐ _____
- ☐ _____
- ☐ _____

Self-Care

Today I'm GRATEFUL for: _____

Today (Small or Great) VICTORIES: _____

Today I LEARNED: _____

NOTES

BRAIN DUMP

What I can control

SELF-CARE IDEAS

HAPPINESS IS

MINDFULNESS DAILY JOURNAL

Date: ___/___/20___   Sun   Mon   Tue   Wed   Thu   Fri   Sat

Today I CHOOSE TO FEEL

Today's FOCUS

Today I FEEL INSPIRED BY

Today's GOOD HABITS

To Do
- [ ]
- [ ]
- [ ]
- [ ]
- [ ]
- [ ]

Self-Care

Today I'm GRATEFUL for: _____

Today (Small or Great) VICTORIES: _____

Today I LEARNED: _____

NOTES

BRAIN DUMP

What I can control

SELF-CARE IDEAS

HAPPINESS IS

MINDFULNESS DAILY JOURNAL

Date: ___/___/20___   Sun   Mon   Tue   Wed   Thu   Fri   Sat

Today I CHOOSE TO FEEL

Today's FOCUS

Today I FEEL INSPIRED BY

Today's GOOD HABITS

To Do

- ☐ _____
- ☐ _____
- ☐ _____
- ☐ _____
- ☐ _____
- ☐ _____

Self-Care

Today I'm GRATEFUL for: _____

Today (Small or Great) VICTORIES: _____

Today I LEARNED: _____

NOTES

BRAIN DUMP

What I can control

SELF-CARE IDEAS

HAPPINESS IS

MINDFULNESS DAILY JOURNAL

Date: ___/___/20___   Sun   Mon   Tue   Wed   Thu   Fri   Sat

Today I CHOOSE TO FEEL

Today's FOCUS

Today I FEEL INSPIRED BY

Today's GOOD HABITS

To Do

Self-Care

Today I'm GRATEFUL for: _____

Today (Small or Great) VICTORIES: _____

Today I LEARNED: _____

NOTES

BRAIN DUMP

What I can control

SELF-CARE IDEAS

HAPPINESS IS

MINDFULNESS DAILY JOURNAL

Date: ___/___/20___   Sun Mon Tue Wed Thu Fri Sat

Today I CHOOSE TO FEEL

Today's FOCUS

Today I FEEL INSPIRED BY

Today's GOOD HABITS

To Do
-
-
-
-
-
-

Self-Care

Today I'm GRATEFUL for: _____

Today (Small or Great) VICTORIES: _____

Today I LEARNED: _____

NOTES

BRAIN DUMP

What I can control

SELF-CARE IDEAS

HAPPINESS IS

MINDFULNESS DAILY JOURNAL

Date: ___/___/20___   Sun   Mon   Tue   Wed   Thu   Fri   Sat

Today I CHOOSE TO FEEL

Today's FOCUS

Today I FEEL INSPIRED BY

Today's GOOD HABITS

To Do

-
-
-
-
-
-

Self-Care

Today I'm GRATEFUL for: _____

Today (Small or Great) VICTORIES: _____

Today I LEARNED: _____

NOTES

BRAIN DUMP

What I can control

SELF-CARE IDEAS

HAPPINESS IS

MINDFULNESS DAILY JOURNAL

Date: ___/___/20___   Sun   Mon   Tue   Wed   Thu   Fri   Sat

Today I CHOOSE TO FEEL

Today's FOCUS

Today I FEEL INSPIRED BY

Today's GOOD HABITS

To Do

- [ ]
- [ ]
- [ ]
- [ ]
- [ ]
- [ ]

Self-Care

Today I'm GRATEFUL for: _____

Today (Small or Great) VICTORIES: _____

Today I LEARNED: _____

NOTES

BRAIN DUMP

What I can control

SELF-CARE IDEAS

HAPPINESS IS

MINDFULNESS DAILY JOURNAL

Date: ___/___/20___   Sun   Mon   Tue   Wed   Thu   Fri   Sat

Today I CHOOSE TO FEEL

Today's FOCUS

Today I FEEL INSPIRED BY

Today's GOOD HABITS

To Do
-
-
-
-
-
-

Self-Care

Today I'm GRATEFUL for: _____

Today (Small or Great) VICTORIES: _____

Today I LEARNED: _____

NOTES

BRAIN DUMP

What I can control

SELF-CARE IDEAS

HAPPINESS IS

MINDFULNESS DAILY JOURNAL

Date: ___/___/20___   Sun Mon Tue Wed Thu Fri Sat

Today I CHOOSE TO FEEL

Today's FOCUS

Today I FEEL INSPIRED BY

Today's GOOD HABITS

To Do
- _____
- _____
- _____
- _____
- _____
- _____

Self-Care

Today I'm GRATEFUL for: _____

Today (Small or Great) VICTORIES: _____

Today I LEARNED: _____

NOTES

BRAIN DUMP

What I can control

SELF-CARE IDEAS

HAPPINESS IS

MINDFULNESS DAILY JOURNAL

Date: ___/___/20___   Sun   Mon   Tue   Wed   Thu   Fri   Sat

Today I CHOOSE TO FEEL

Today's FOCUS

Today I FEEL INSPIRED BY

Today's GOOD HABITS

To Do

-
-
-
-
-
-

Self-Care

Today I'm GRATEFUL for: _____

Today (Small or Great) VICTORIES: _____

Today I LEARNED: _____

NOTES

BRAIN DUMP

What I can control

SELF-CARE IDEAS

HAPPINESS IS

MINDFULNESS DAILY JOURNAL

Date: ___/___/20___   Sun   Mon   Tue   Wed   Thu   Fri   Sat

Today I CHOOSE TO FEEL

Today's FOCUS

Today I FEEL INSPIRED BY

Today's GOOD HABITS

To Do
- [ ]
- [ ]
- [ ]
- [ ]
- [ ]
- [ ]

Self-Care

Today I'm GRATEFUL for: _____

Today (Small or Great) VICTORIES: _____

Today I LEARNED: _____

NOTES

BRAIN DUMP

What I can control

SELF-CARE IDEAS

HAPPINESS IS

MINDFULNESS DAILY JOURNAL

Date: ___/___/20___   Sun   Mon   Tue   Wed   Thu   Fri   Sat

Today I CHOOSE TO FEEL

Today's FOCUS

Today I FEEL INSPIRED BY

Today's GOOD HABITS

To Do

- [ ]
- [ ]
- [ ]
- [ ]
- [ ]
- [ ]

Self-Care

Today I'm GRATEFUL for: _____

Today (Small or Great) VICTORIES: _____

Today I LEARNED: _____

NOTES

BRAIN DUMP

What I can control

SELF-CARE IDEAS

HAPPINESS IS

MINDFULNESS DAILY JOURNAL

Date: ___/___/20___   Sun Mon Tue Wed Thu Fri Sat

Today I CHOOSE TO FEEL

Today's FOCUS

Today I FEEL INSPIRED BY

Today's GOOD HABITS

To Do
- [ ]
- [x]
- [ ]
- [ ]
- [ ]
- [ ]

Self-Care

Today I'm GRATEFUL for: _____

Today (Small or Great) VICTORIES: _____

Today I LEARNED: _____

NOTES

BRAIN DUMP

What I can control

SELF-CARE IDEAS

HAPPINESS IS

MINDFULNESS DAILY JOURNAL

Date: ___/___/20___   Sun   Mon   Tue   Wed   Thu   Fri   Sat

Today I CHOOSE TO FEEL

Today's FOCUS

Today I FEEL INSPIRED BY

Today's GOOD HABITS

To Do

☐ _____
☐ _____
☐ _____
☐ _____
☐ _____
☐ _____

Self-Care

Today I'm GRATEFUL for: _____

Today (Small or Great) VICTORIES: _____

Today I LEARNED: _____

NOTES

BRAIN DUMP

What I can control

SELF-CARE IDEAS

HAPPINESS IS

MINDFULNESS DAILY JOURNAL

Date: ___/___/20___   Sun   Mon   Tue   Wed   Thu   Fri   Sat

Today I CHOOSE TO FEEL

Today's FOCUS

Today I FEEL INSPIRED BY

Today's GOOD HABITS

To Do

-
-
-
-
-
-

Self-Care

Today I'm GRATEFUL for: _____

Today (Small or Great) VICTORIES: _____

Today I LEARNED: _____

NOTES

BRAIN DUMP

What I can control

SELF-CARE IDEAS

HAPPINESS IS

MINDFULNESS DAILY JOURNAL

Date: ___/___/20___   Sun Mon Tue Wed Thu Fri Sat

Today I CHOOSE TO FEEL

Today's FOCUS

Today I FEEL INSPIRED BY

Today's GOOD HABITS

To Do
- [ ]
- [ ]
- [ ]
- [ ]
- [ ]
- [ ]

Self-Care

Today I'm GRATEFUL for: _____

Today (Small or Great) VICTORIES: _____

Today I LEARNED: _____

NOTES

BRAIN DUMP

What I can control

SELF-CARE IDEAS

HAPPINESS IS

MINDFULNESS DAILY JOURNAL

Date: ___/___/20___   Sun   Mon   Tue   Wed   Thu   Fri   Sat

Today I CHOOSE TO FEEL

Today's FOCUS

Today I FEEL INSPIRED BY

Today's GOOD HABITS

To Do
- ☐ _____
- ☐ _____
- ☐ _____
- ☐ _____
- ☐ _____
- ☐ _____

Self-Care
_____
_____
_____
_____
_____
_____

Today I'm GRATEFUL for: _____

Today (Small or Great) VICTORIES: _____

Today I LEARNED: _____

NOTES

BRAIN DUMP

What I can control

SELF-CARE IDEAS

HAPPINESS IS

MINDFULNESS DAILY JOURNAL

Date: ___/___/20___   Sun   Mon   Tue   Wed   Thu   Fri   Sat

Today I CHOOSE TO FEEL

Today's FOCUS

Today I FEEL INSPIRED BY

Today's GOOD HABITS

To Do
-
-
-
-
-
-

Self-Care

Today I'm GRATEFUL for: _____

Today (Small or Great) VICTORIES: _____

Today I LEARNED: _____

NOTES

BRAIN DUMP

What I can control

SELF-CARE IDEAS

HAPPINESS IS

Printed in Great Britain
by Amazon